FEMALE SINGERS OF THE 1950'S

PIANO / VOCAL / GUITAR

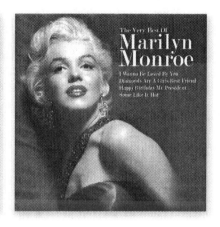

Catalog No. 44042
ISBN 978-1-922657-53-0

Produced by John L. Haag

Sales and Shipping:
Professional Music Institute LLC
1336 Cruzero Street, Box 128
Ojai, California 93024

LILLO'S MUSIC
10848-82 AVE. N.W.
EDMONTON, ALBERTA
T6E 2B3
TEL.: 780-433-0138

Female Singers of the 1950's

PIANO / VOCAL / GUITAR

FEMALE SINGERS OF THE 1950'S

PIANO / VOCAL / GUITAR   *continued*

4

Allegheny Moon

Lyric and Music by
Dick Manning and Al Hoffman

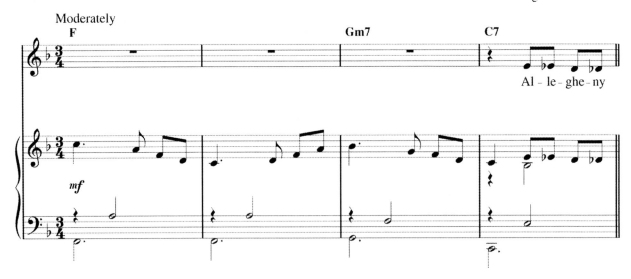

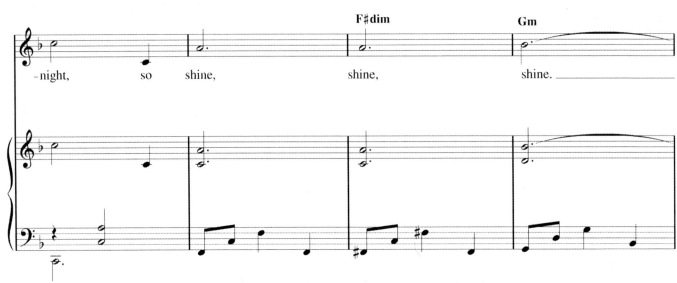

Allegheny moon 2-3

6

Allegheny moon 3-3

Botch - A - Me
(Ba-Ba-Baciami Piccina)

English lyric and music adapted by Eddie Y. Stanley
Italian lyric and music by R. Morbelli and L. Astore

8

Cross Over The Bridge

Lyric and Music by
George David Weiss and Bennie Benjamin

Moderately Slow with a Beat

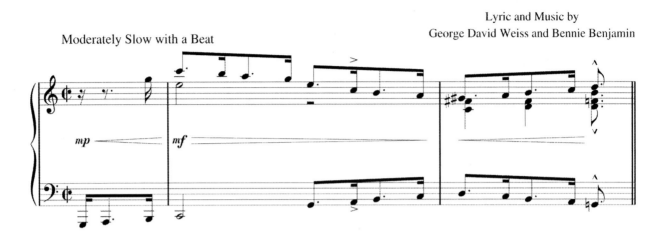

1. If you're a guy who's had a gal in each and ev – 'ry port, and
2. (If) you have built a boat to take you to the green – er side, and
3. (I) know it is – n't eas – y to re – sist temp – ta – tion's call, but

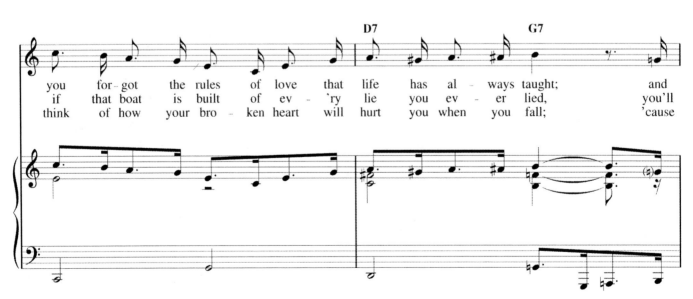

you for – got the rules of love that life has al – ways taught; and
if that boat is built of ev – 'ry lie you ev – er lied, you'll
think of how your bro – ken heart will hurt you when you fall; 'cause

if you broke as man - y hearts as rip - ples in a stream, well,
nev - er reach the prom - ised land of love, I guar - an - tee; 'cause
some day you will find that you are hope - less - ly in love, and

broth - er, here's the on - ly way that you can be re - deemed!
lies can - not hold wa - ter, and you'll sink in - to the sea!
she'll be - long to some - one else as sure as stars a - bove!

Refrain

Cross o - ver tha bridge! Cross o - ver the bridge! Change your

reck - less way of liv - ing. Cross o - ver the bridge! Leave your

fick - le past be - hind you,___ and true ro - mance will find you, brother! Cross o - ver the

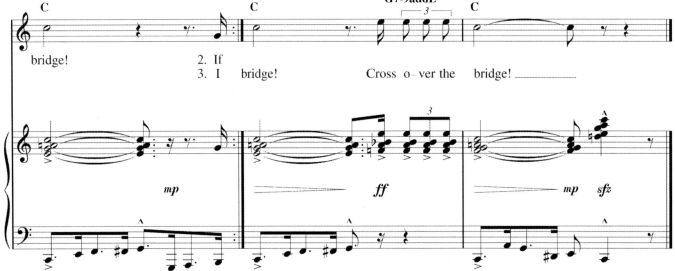

bridge!

2. If
3. I bridge! Cross o - ver the bridge!___

Dark Moon

Lyric and Music by
Ned Miller

high up in the sky, Oh, tell me why, oh tell me, why you've lost your

splendor. Dark moon, _____ What is the

cause your light withdraws, Is it be - cause, is it be - cause I've lost my

love? love? _____

Dark moon 3-3

Diamonds Are A Girl's Best Friend

Lyric by Leo Robin
Music by Jule Styne

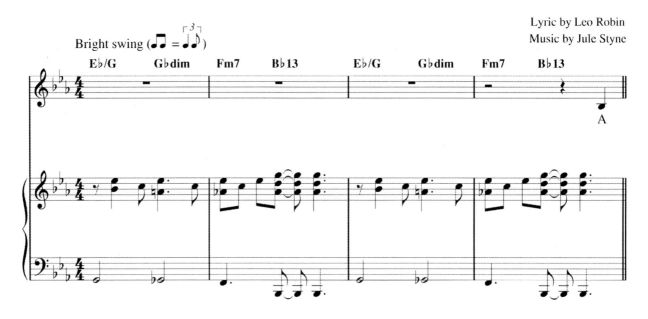

kiss on the hand may be quite con - ti - nen - tal, but
may come a time when a lass needs a law - yer, but

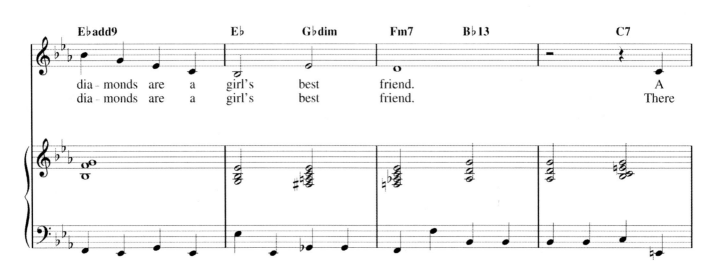

dia - monds are a girl's best friend.
dia - monds are a girl's best friend.
A
There

18

Everybody Loves A Lover

Note: The 1st 16 bars of the Chorus and Refrain
may be sung and played simultaneously, as a duet.

Lyric by Richard Adler
Music by Robert Allen

20

A Guy Is A Guy

Lyric and Music by
Oscar Brand

24

A guy is a guy 3-3

How Important Can It Be ?

Lyric and Music by
George David Weiss and Bennie Benjamin

Slowly and Expressively

How im-por-tant can it be that I tast-ed oth-er lips?

That was long be-fore you came to me with the won-der of your kiss!

So the sto-ry got a-round of an old ro-mance and me;

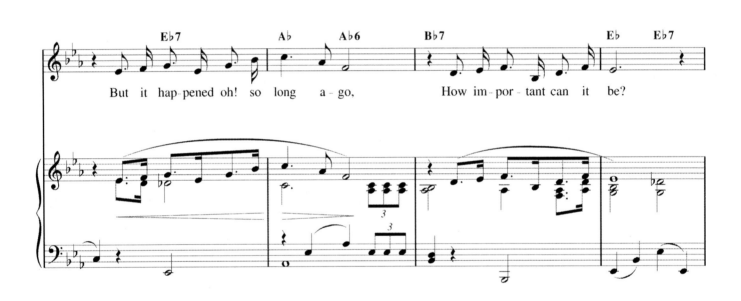

But it hap-pened oh! so long a-go, How im-por-tant can it be?

Mine was a young and a fool – ish heart, seek-ing love at ev – 'ry turn;

How Much Is That Doggie In The Window ?

Lyric and Music by
Bob Merrill

32

How much is that doggie in the window ? 5-5

It's A Most Unusual Day

Lyric by Harold Adamson
Music by Jimmy McHugh

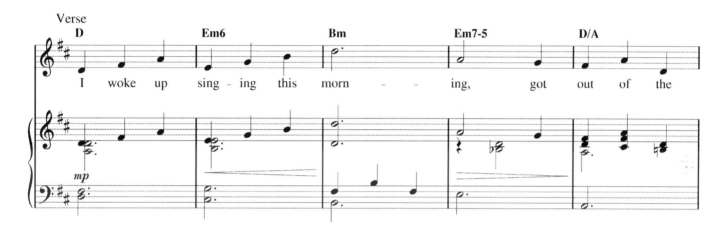

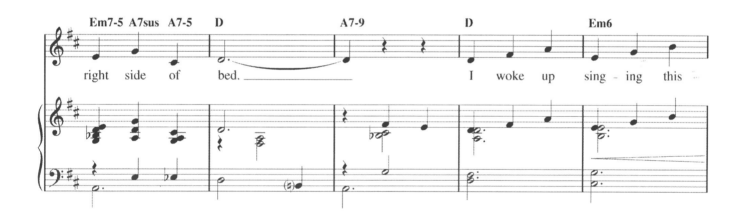

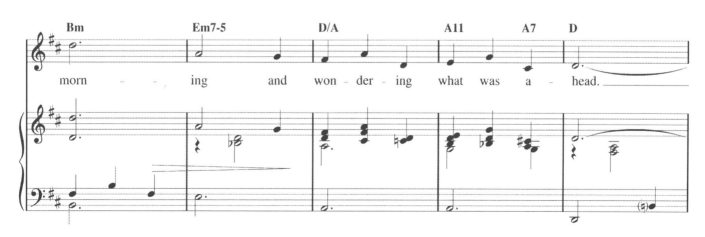

34

It's a most unusual day 3-5

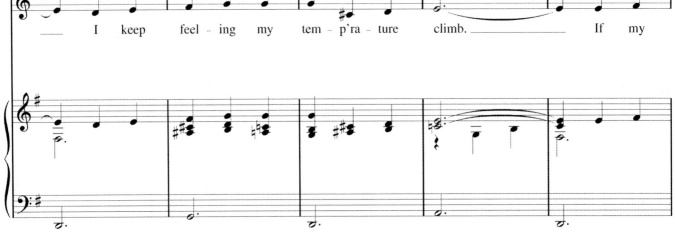

It's a most unusual day 5-5

It's So Nice To Have A Man Around The House

Lyric by Jack M. Elliot
Music by Harold Spina

3rd Chorus

It's so nice to have a man around the house,
Oh, so nice to have a man around the house,
Just a hero bold and vicious,
Who'll insist he get his wishes,
Oh, but first he'll do the dishes... It's so nice.
Oh, a house is just a house without a man,
He's the necessary evil in your plan;
Just a knight in shining armor,
Who is something of a charmer,
Though it's two to one you wind up with a louse,
It's so nice to have a man around the house.

4th Chorus

It's so nice to have a man around the house,
Oh, so nice to have a man around the house,
Just a guy who is attentive,
And who has a strong incentive,
To be more or less inventive...It's so nice.
Oh, a house is just a house without a man,
He's the necessary evil in your plan,
So put no one else above him,
When you love him really love him,
Even though he may be someone'else's spouse,
It's so nice to have a man around the house.

Make Yourself Comfortable

Lyric and Music by
Bob Merrill

Memories Of You

Lyric by Andy Razaf
Music by Eubie Blake

Why can't I for-get like I should? Hea-ven knows I would if I could, but I just can't
Tho' for years we've been far a-part, Time heals ev-'ry-thing but my heart, That still aches for

keep you off my mind _____ Tho' you've gone, and love was in vain.
you the same old way _____ Seems I can't es-cape from the past,

All a-round me you still re-main, Won-der why fate should be so un-kind: _____
And your spell keeps hold-ing me fast, Each to-mor-row is like yes-ter-day: _____

44

Memories of you 3-3

Mambo Italiano

Lyric and Music by
Bob Merrill

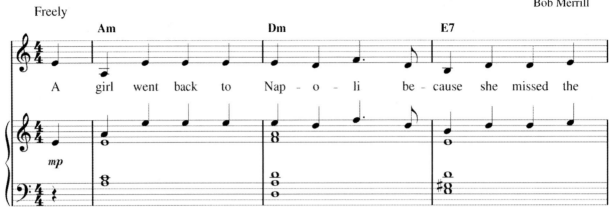

A girl went back to Nap – o – li be – cause she missed the

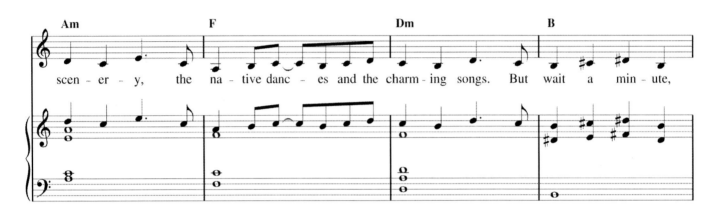

scen – er – y, the na – tive danc – es and the charm – ing songs. But wait a min – ute,

something's wrong.

Hey mam – bo, mam – bo I – tal – i – an – o

Instrumental

Mambo italiano 2-4

48

May You Always

Lyric and Music by
Larry Marks and Dick Charles

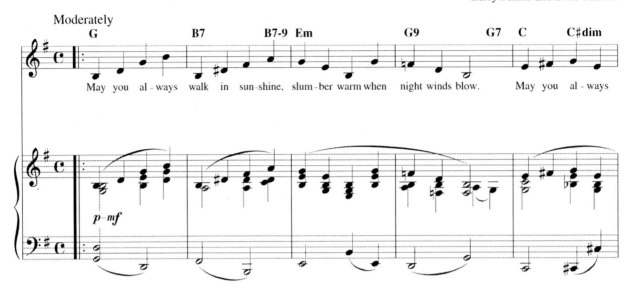

May you al-ways walk in sun-shine, slum-ber warm when night winds blow. May you al-ways

live with laugh-ter for a smile be-comes you so. May good for-tune find your door-way,

may the blue-bird sing your song. May no trou-ble trav-el your way, may no wor-ry stay too long.

Mockin' Bird Hill

Lyric and Music by
Vaughan Horton

54

Mockin' bird hill 3-3

Mr. Wonderful

(From The Musical "Mr. Wonderful")

Lyric and Music by
George David Weiss, Jerry Bock and Larry Holofcener

Why this feel - ing? _____ Why this glow?

Why the thrill when you say, "Hel - lo!"? _____

56

58

Oh! there's much more ____ I could say, ____
But the words keep slip - ping a - way; ____
And I'm left with on - ly one point of view: ____
Mis - ter Won - der - ful, ____ that's you! ____

Mr. Wonderful 5-5

Music! Music! Music!

(Put Another Nickel In)

Lyric and Music by
Stephan Weiss and Bernie Baum

Put an-oth-er nick-el in, ___ in the nick-el-o-de-on ___

All I want is hav-ing you ___ and Mu-sic! Mu-sic! Mus-sic!

Ricochet Romance

Lyric and Music by
Norman Gimbel, Larry Coleman and Joe Darion

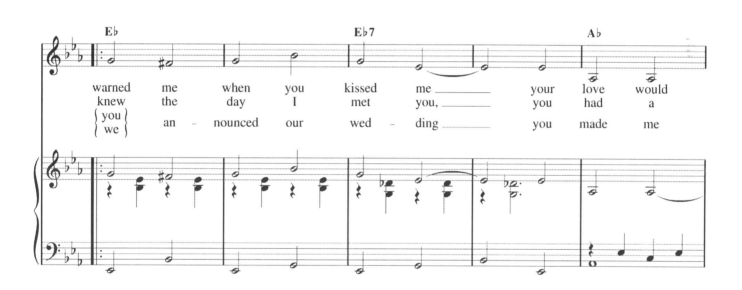

64

My Happiness

Lyric by Betty Peterson
Music by Borney Bergantine

My Heart Cries For You

Lyric by Carl Sigman
Music by Percy Faith

If you're in Ar-i-zo-na I'll fol-low you, If
bloom has left the ros-es since you left me, The

you're in Min-ne-so-ta I'll be there too. You'll have a mil-lion
birds have left my win-dow since you left me. I'm lone-ly as a

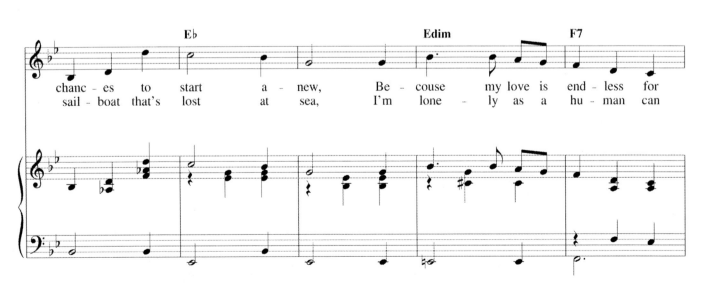

chanc-es to start a new, Be-couse my love is end-less for
sail-boat that's lost at sea, I'm lone-ly as a hu-man can

My heart cries for you 2-2

Pledging My Love

Lyric and Music by
Ferdinand "Fats" Washington and Don Robey

Pledging my love 2-2

Sentimental Journey

Lyric and Music by
Bud Green, Les Brown and Ben Homer

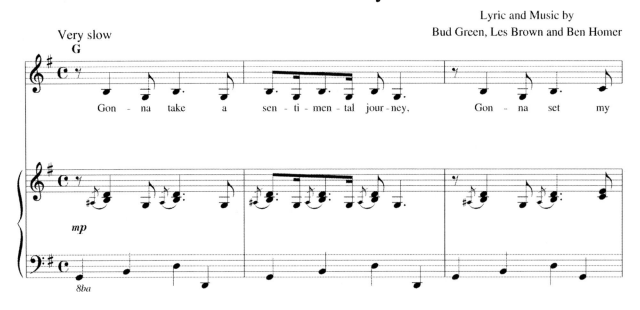

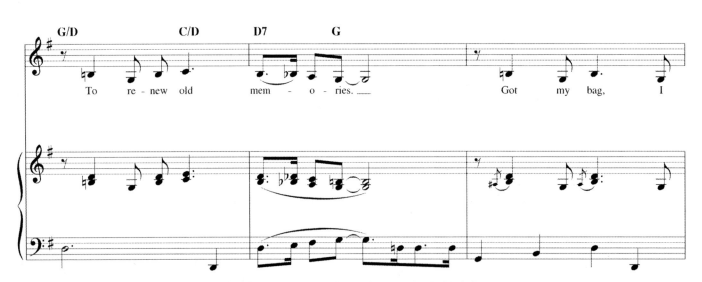

74

Sentimental journey 3-3

Teach Me Tonight

Lyric by Sammy Cahn
Music by Gene DePaul

Teach me tonight 2-3

A Sweet Old Fashioned Girl

Lyric and Music by
Bob Merrill

Wouldn't an-y-bo-dy care to meet a sweet old fashioned girl? Skoobelee doobeedum, Doesn't

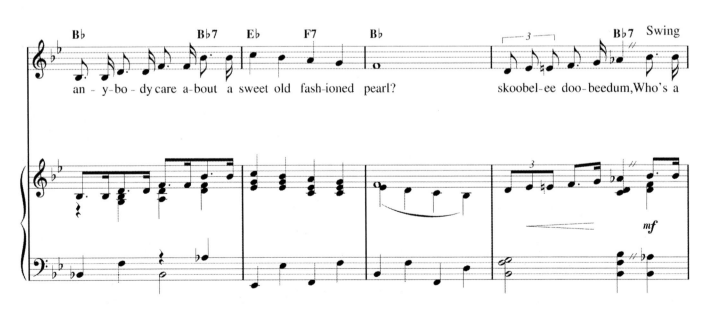

an-y-bo-dy care a-bout a sweet old fash-ioned pearl? skoobel-ee doo-beedum, Who's a

There Goes My Heart

Lyric by Benny Davis
Music by Abner Silver

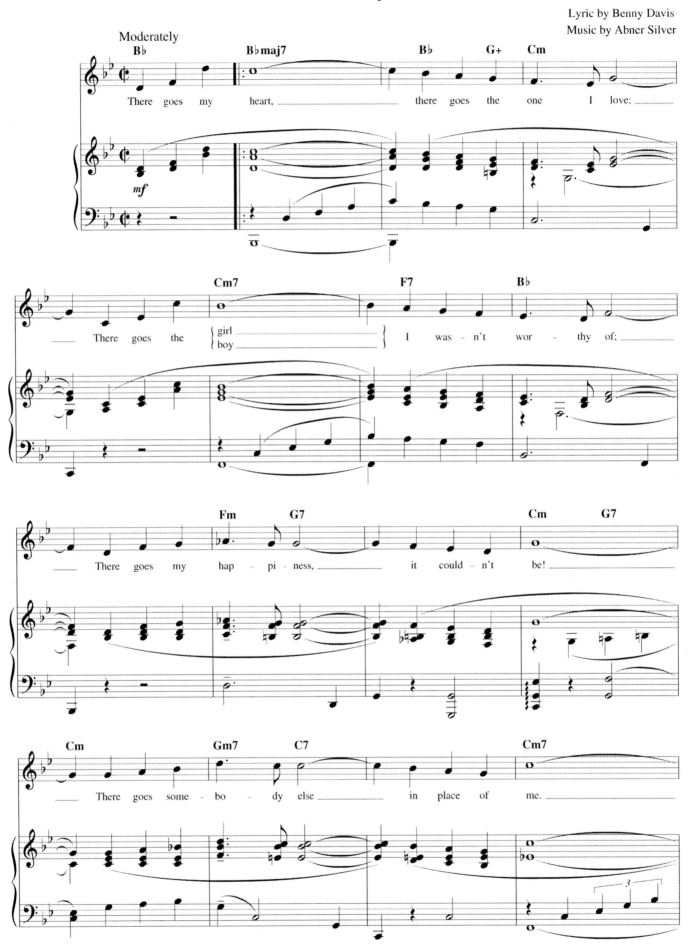

There goes my heart 2-2

This Ole House

Lyric and Music by
Stuart Hamblen

85

This ole house 2-6

This ole house 3-6

This ole house 4-6

This ole house 6-6

Too Young To Go Steady

Lyric by Harold Adamson
Music by Jimmy McHugh

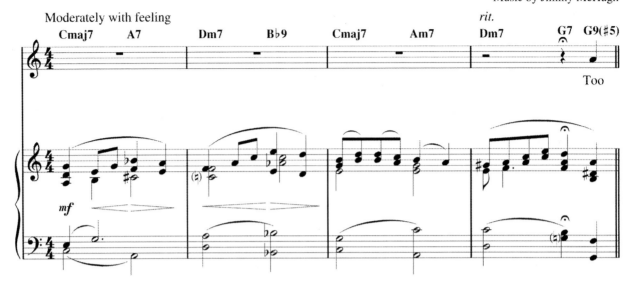

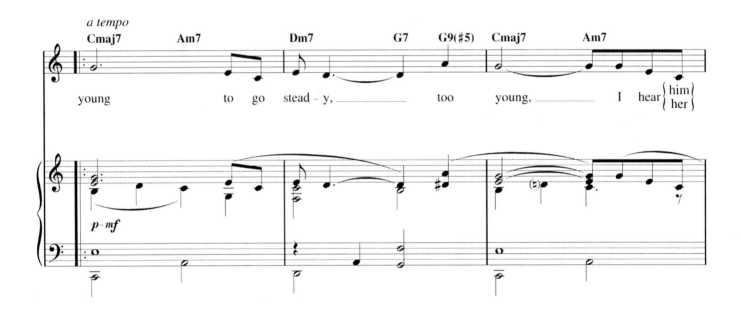

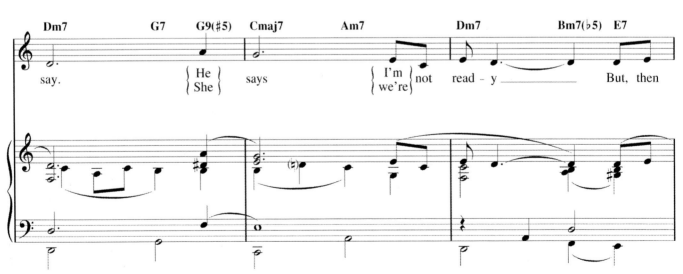

92

Too young to go steady 3-3

Vaya Con Dios
(May God Be With You)

Lyric and Music by
Larry Russell, Inez James and Buddy Pepper

94

Vaya con Dios 2-4

96

Vaya con Dios 4-4

Vaya Con Dios

Lyric and Music by
Larry Russell, Inez James and Buddy Pepper

Vaya con Dios mi vida
Vaya con Dios mi amor

Se llegó ya el momento de separarnos
En silencio el corazón dice y suspira

Vaya con Dios mi vida
Vaya con Dios mi amor

Las campanas de la iglesia suenan tristes
Y parece que al sonar también te dicen

Vaya con Dios mi vida
Vaya con Dios mi amor

Adonde vayas tu, yo iré contigo
En sueños siempre junto a ti estaré
Mi voz escucharás, dulce amor mío
Pensando como yo estarás
Volvernos siempre a ver

La alborada al despertar feliz te espera
Si en tu corazón yo voy a donde quiera

Vaya con Dios mi vida
Vaya con Dios mi amor
Vaya con Dios mi vida
Vaya con Dios mi amor

What A Diff'rence A Day Made

(Cuando Vuelva A Tu Lado)

Lyric by Stanley Adams
Music by Maria Grever

What a diff'rence a day made 2-3

Why Don't You Believe Me ?

Lyric and Music by Lew Douglas,
Luther King Laney and Leroy W. Rodde

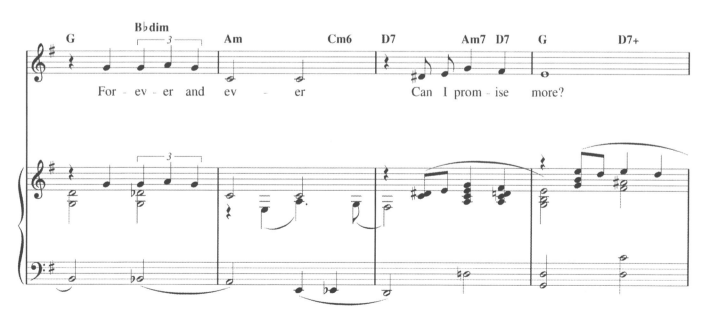

Here, __ is a heart, __ for you on - ly, That you can keep or break.

How else can I tell you What more can I do

Why don't you be - lieve me I love on - ly you. you.

Who's Sorry Now ?

Lyric by Harry Ruby and Bert Kalmar
Music by Ted Snyder

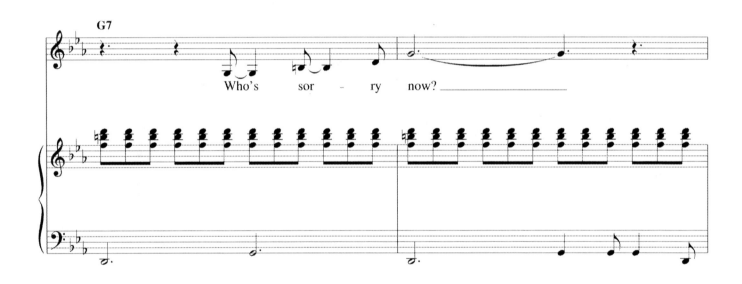

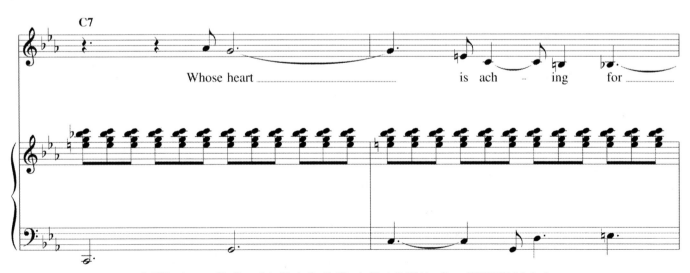

F7

break - ing _____ each ___ vow. ___

Bb7

Who's sad   and   blue? _____

Eb

Who's cry - ing   too? _____

Bb   F7

Just   like   I   cried

Wheel Of Fortune

Lyric and Music by
George David Weiss and Bennie Benjamin

The wheel of for - tune _____ goes spin-ning a-

-round; _____ will the ar - row point my way?

Will this _____ be the day _____ Oh! Wheel of